The Gospel of Anonymous

Absolving All Men of the Most Hideous Crime of Deicide

László Bitó

iUniverse, Inc.
Bloomington

The Gospel of Anonymous
Absolving All Men of the Most Hideous Crime of Deicide

iUniverse books may be ordered through booksellers or by contacting:

iUniverse
1663 Liberty Drive
Bloomington, IN 47403
www.iuniverse.com
1-800-Authors (1-800-288-4677)

Because of the dynamic nature of the Internet, any web addresses or links contained in
this book may have changed since publication and may no longer be valid.

Any people depicted in stock imagery provided by Thinkstock are models,
and such images are being used for illustrative purposes only.

Certain stock imagery © Thinkstock.

ISBN: 978-1-4620-0205-4 (sc)
ISBN: 978-1-4620-0207-8 (dj)
ISBN: 978-1-4620-0206-1 (ebk)

Printed in the United States of America

iUniverse rev. date: 5/6/2011

Part I
Our Time and
Environs

The Preamble of
the Witness

I met Yeshua of Nazareth in the troubled years
of my youth and became, for the rest of my life,
his true and faithful disciple. His example and
words saved me from the darkness of youth's
tumults and brought joy and understanding to
a life nearly lost. All I have become I owe to
him.

You may, in your time, know Yeshua better as
the prophet of compassion and love, or perhaps
as Jesus, as he began to be called by those of his
followers who disregarded his admonition that
his kingdom is not of this world and followed
their thirst for worldly power to Rome.

If you wonder why I had to write this testimony,
it is enough to know that after two peaceful
years as a disciple of Yeshua of Nazareth, I was
for most of my remaining days either a witness

or a victim of conflicts. I must now write in order to understand and help resolve how the teachings of love and compassion could lead to such often murderous discord.

I will tell you about the persecution of the disciples by Saul who later became Paul, and there were many others who were convinced that we, the disciples of Yeshua the Nazarene, had no other aspiration or aim than to corrupt the faith of our forefathers – this in spite of the fact that Yeshua wanted us to live by the essence of the Torah. True, not by its words, which had been cast into immutable writing long ago, at times very different from ours. This is why Yeshua did not let us commit his words to writing; he believed in the wise teaching that a day on which we have left nothing behind is a day wasted, as is a day on which we have failed to open ourselves to something new. Even the greatest thoughts of today become monuments to the past as soon as they have sunk into the thirsty leaves of papyrus.

I see with increasing clarity that misrepresentations of events and teachings will set generations to come against one another, releasing beasts more dreadful than ever dreamt in the worst nightmares of the begetters of the story of the apocalypse. This dismal future was revealed to me in my contemplations – forced on me by the accumulation of years that corrupts the body but broadens the horizons of the mind, sometimes even allowing us a taste of the wisdom that evaded us through the sufferings of our youth, so that in the brief time remaining to us we may know its comforts, and its torments.

With a heart heavy with sorrow, I have already seen many conflicts taking root among us: between the very brethren of Yeshua and his followers of different bloodlines and persuasions. I shall mention some of them in *odium introductum* that caused me much personal anguish and pain, but bear with me, for my Gospel is about much more, about a looming danger that may, I fear, cast a dark shadow of the ghastly, vile, and repugnant accusation of Deicide over your life as well, however far in the future you might live.

I must set the record straight on this abomination, because nothing would sadden my beloved master more than to discover that the sufferings he bore out of love have been used to sow the seeds of suspicion and hatred. Yet, because I cannot know how much of the present will be remembered in the future, when this writing finds you, I must bring you into the time and place in which this scroll was labored into being.

The Disciples of
Yeshua in Rome

The supporters of Peter – who always imagined himself to be the first among the disciples of Yeshua – settled in Rome, not upon instruction from the Master, but, on the contrary, they went there hoping that Peter himself or his successors would establish his throne at the seat of the Empire.

The desire to conquer Rome had already, in our days, led to the death of hundreds on the cross – or thousands, if we believe the accounts of those who want history to remember Nero as the bloodiest emperor to rule in the City of Romulus. Such exaggerated numbers can also be attributed to Peter's adherents, who believe martyrdom to be the shortest road to heaven. He, who is said to have denied Yeshua three times, encouraged others to let themselves be thrown to the lions in testimony to their faith and as an example for others to follow. This, in the name of our Master who offered his own life to save hundreds of Zealots from certain martyrdom as they were readying to free Judea from Rome's yoke.

But the passions I feel against these perversions of my Master's teachings have me running too far ahead of the story that yet awaits telling.

Why My Gospel Is Not Found among the Other Scrolls of Our Times

Because of my commitment to remain faithful to our Master's words, as I heard them with my own ears, and to his deeds, as I saw them with my own eyes, none of my writings were accepted by Paul.

You may know well this properly circumcised Jew and devoted citizen of Rome, who became Peter's partner in laying the foundation of what I fear will become the new *Religio Romana*, a new domain of uncircumcised pagans, baptized in the name of the creed "there shall be one fold and one shepherd," which they quote more often than any of the other teachings of the Master. As I make this accusation, I remember fondly how Yeshua urged us to go forth two by two, in pairs, to spread his word after he left us, and to take nothing for our journey: no scrip, no bread, no coins in our purses.

I understood him to say that we should remain humble even in the glory of the demand to be heard by so many, not building another hierarchy of Levites and priests. I therefore interpret the Master's words to mean that we should not have one shepherd who will inevitably raise himself above the fold, distinguishing himself with purchases of silks and gold, spending more of the tithes on the households and glory of high priests than on the alms of the poor.

The Conquest of the Flock by Paul, Who Used to Be Saul

Yeshua did say that he has other sheep who must hear his words, but he never said that they should hear only what Paul decided to allow into the scrolls of teachings that he began to call *Evangelion,* meaning Good Tidings, Godspel, or Gospel.

This Paul was called Saul of Tarsus in the days when he was delivering many of us, true followers of Yeshua, to Pilate or Herod, the henchmen of Rome. I was among the last of his many victims before, on his way to Damascus, he allegedly saw Yeshua in the heat of the day in an apparition. According to his own account, he recognized him at once, even though he had never seen him before. He believed he had heard Yeshua's voice saying: "Saul, Saul, why persecutest thou me?" Those who were with him did not hear the voice, and I was not there to witness what happened.

Undeniably, this Saul became Paul when he recognized that he could achieve greater power and vainglory as the leader of Yeshua's followers than he could as their executioner. And the fact is that Paul would not allow me to write my own gospel, according to what I had witnessed. Therefore, my name will mean nothing to those of you who in times to come may – if the Lord wills – find and read my modest contribution to history's truths.

On My Compulsion to Write This True Account

Why then, you may ask, do I commit my thoughts, engendered by years of painful contemplation, to parchment? I am not writing for tomorrow of a wound so raw that it is still painful to the touch. And it may well be that I am not even writing for others. It may well be that this scroll will never be read by anyone. I am writing these lines between bouts of often agonizing contemplation because I need to understand how the gentle teachings of our Master led to so much conflict between Jews and baptized Jews, and between them and all the Gentiles, baptized or pagan.

As I have already mentioned, I not only witnessed the persecution of those who lived by the teachings of Yeshua, but was a victim myself, and indeed was nearly felled by the unfathomably vicious hatred that Saul harbored against us: circumcised and uncircumcised followers of Yeshua alike. And this happened not much more than a year after I witnessed the conflict between Aramaic and Greek-speaking baptized Jews, leading to the mortal stoning of Stephan.

A few years later, we, the baptized disciples of Yeshua, stood side by side with Sadducee and Pharisee Jews to prevent pagan legionnaires from desecrating the Temple by erecting, on the order of Caligula, his statue. And was it the Almighty who struck him down – as many say – before his diabolic plan could be completed? But not before I fell into bondage and was dragged to Rome in chains. And there were many defenders who perished on the cross. I considered them the lucky ones, as I faced a much slower, more agonizing death under the heavy yoke of slavery. But as it turned out, as a slave, I escaped banishment under the order of Claudius, who grew increasingly fed up with the conflicts between baptized and non-baptized Jews that repeatedly flared into violent confrontations in the squalor of the Transtevere ghetto.

As I witnessed, and for the most part suffered through, this senseless cruelty of men against men, you should not judge me too harshly if it became my obsession to try to find its origins. Many sleepless nights, chained to a post after a grueling day at the quarry, I lay on my back, overwhelmed by the star-studded sky, and prayed to the Almighty: *Oh, Lord, who surrounds us with so much beauty and planted so much good in us, as was revealed to us by your son, Yeshua, how can you allow us to be as cruel to one another as I have had to behold since he left us?*

My Escape from Bondage
and Fall into an Abyss
of Foreboding

I had all but given up hope, when word of my desperation reached a few of those with whom I had shared our Master's last supper in Jerusalem, and they broke my chains and helped me escape from servitude. They did so after I swore to them that I would not reveal their deed to Paul, who had become increasingly careful not to offend his newfound Roman friends.

I will not, therefore, commit the shameful sin of ingratitude and turn against those who gave me refuge. Yet I feel compelled to commit to writing for eternity the truth of why our Master chose the fate that you all may read about in the Gospels compiled to serve Paul's goal of sowing the seeds of an empire greater than any Caesar had ever dreamed of – an empire that can be achieved only by welcoming into this "one fold" uncircumcised pagans of all sorts and accepting their customs and rites, their feasts and their need to worship and serve multiple gods. This worries me to no end, as it leads us astray from the simple community of loving equals that was envisioned and advocated by our Yeshua.

The Concerns and Angst
of Yeshua's Brethren
in Jerusalem

Paul insists that it is for the good of all to have one fold, ruled not by the sword, but by faith. And by him, who insists that he is not worthy even to stand in Peter's shadow, but actually it is Paul's shadow that engulfs us all, including Yeshua's followers in Jerusalem. They, including Yeshua's half-brother, James, argued in vain against allowing uncircumcised pagans into our flock. In my mind, these concerns had already proved to be well founded, because the lately admitted pagan younger brothers show all signs of feeling inferior to us, and will always be envious of us, their circumcised elder brethren, because they cannot share our covenant with the Almighty. And, as we all know, envy begets hatred, and hatred often finds pretext for murder, as exemplified by the story of Cain and Abel, as we know it.

As a survivor of the revolt against Rome, I am against the forging of swords for people to kill one another. But how long could faith maintain peace if the Holy Scriptures promulgated by Paul include stories that place the blame of deicide on Yeshua's own people?

Why I Must Commit
the Truth to Writing,
and Yet Hide It Away

This is why I am committing these truths to writing for those in the distant future who will be ready to seek them, beyond the words bequeathed to them by Paul and his followers, and search for a deeper understanding of the true meaning of the teachings and deeds of Yeshua. In the time allotted me in my old age, I can only hope to tell you the true story of what led to the suffering and crucifixion of our Master. I do so in the hope that, when by the will of the Lord it is found, this story will set you on the right path to end the animosity between the older and the younger brothers.

Unfortunately, false teachings originating in man's infinite imagination can be more seductive than truths limited to the much smaller world of the possible. The truth about the son of a carpenter who stood out among all other sons of Israel only in his great love and understanding of his fellow men does not grip the imagination of the pagans of this empire. They live in a fantasy world of mythical gods and goddesses who consort with beasts and men alike and do not obey the laws of nature.

This is why Paul favors the more fantastic stories about Yeshua, which attribute to him deeds so miraculous they puzzle the imagination. I cannot contribute to these, as I saw his immense love and empathy, which alone explain his power to heal. And I believe that a time will come when people will recognize that there is no greater miracle than the love that radiated from our Master and can be possessed by all of us who follow his true teachings. There is no story that stands better witness to this love of his than the true account of his freeing of his lifelong friend from the prison of Pilate.

This is why I came in secret to this cave to write this testimony of his great love. I will seal my gospel into a pottery urn that I intend to bury in the sand of the desert, that it may only surface in the distant future when there may be a greater need for, and acceptance of, the truth.

When it will surface I cannot venture to say. The waves of sand move thousands of times more slowly than those of the sea. Where once there were dunes, in hundreds of years there will be valleys laying bare times past. I will dig my urn deep enough into the sand to keep it hidden for centuries, rather than decades.

Why I Don't Expect to Find Open Minds among My Contemporaries

We have come a long way from the more blissful times when we – most of the disciples of the Master – were living in Jerusalem and its surroundings and were cherishing his memory by sharing amongst ourselves our most precious recollections of him. There were, of course, those among us who remembered things that had never happened, but could have happened. And later on, these of our brothers came up with stories that could not have happened. These embellishments did not much bother those of us who sought to guard the purity of his memory and the authenticity of his teachings, until we learned that one of them had written down everything he had heard, or remembered hearing, or his own loving fantasy had conjured

up about the miraculous deeds of the One whom
we all missed so much.

I must confess that one of his stories brought
me to tears, even though its account of the
miraculous healing of a child never happened.
We did not mind listening to or reading our
friend's heartrending tales and enlightening
parables, which we all knew to be the products
of his big heart and rich imagination. And even
if we knew that they had never taken place, they
illustrated wonderfully Yeshua's great empathy
toward all those in need of his love.

The First Written Story of Yeshua's Life Arrives in Rome, Where It Vanishes

We only began to worry when this scribe went to Rome at the invitation of Paul and we heard that soon after he arrived there with his scrolls he disappeared. So many years later, no one knows – or perhaps no one dares say – what became of his scrolls. I tried to find out after I had been freed from servitude, and I was compelled to conclude that they had vanished long before. I suspected that they might have been taken by Paul, because what he wanted to believe to be true, our friend in his honesty clearly indicated to be fantasy: not to document a truth, but rather to illustrate it.

I cannot be certain how many scribes copied parts of these scrolls or based their own embellishments on it, but judging from the very different appearance and language of the different scrolls and fragments I have seen in Rome, they must have come from well over a dozen hands. And most of these authors or copying scribes must have seen the scrolls that came from Jerusalem, the very scrolls I was searching for.

Some of the scribes with whom I managed to meet even admitted this, referring to the author of their only source of information about the Master as *Quedam,* not even knowing that it is not a name, but simply means "someone" in the language of the native Romans, which most scribes apparently did not know. Moreover, most of the copying scribes were not even fluent in Greek, judging from the mistakes they made. But these scrolls were in great demand, and more than a few scribes improved their fortunes by them, especially those who conjured up parts more miraculous than anyone had before.

A poor soul showed me a fragment of an early gospel he had obtained for a week's wages. He cherished these few lines, although he worshiped Mithras and kept his rites even after he had been baptized with water, just as he had been baptized with the blood of a bull many years earlier, when in his youth he had become a legionary. Moreover, this treasured piece was written in Greek, a language that he, a barbarian from up north, did not speak. But it did not matter to him anyway, since he could not read any language, a fatal shortcoming that he shared with most of the uncircumcised recruits of Peter and Paul.

Why Some Writings Had to Be Destroyed: A Word in Defense of Paul

This writing is for the distant future, not to add to the confusion of the many contradictory and sometimes preposterous stories of our days, such as the one describing in flowery language how every young woman whose eyes met with Yeshua's fell into ecstasy and conceived his child.

So you can see that Paul and his men had a good reason to confiscate and destroy such writings. My only objection is that his selection of what to accept was biased against Yeshua's brethren, against his own people. The most devastating example of this is the Gospel of Matthew, the former tax collector, who, describing the events leading to the crucifixion of our Master, has the Jews jeering, "Let his blood be upon us and upon our children."

It pains me to think what these untruths may bring upon us in the future. What kinds of hatreds may they fire? Yet I am powerless to contradict these scribes openly, for they enjoy the protection of Paul, whose cause they serve with such devastating falsehoods.

The Foresight of Mary of Magdala and the Miracle of Bread and Fish

I refer only to the men, because no words were bequeathed to us by Mary Magdalene, who knew more than any of us about Yeshua – especially about his earlier years. It was Magdalene, for example, who, not long after the beheading of John of the Jordan, told the crowd who came to listen to the Master to bring food for themselves: bread and dried fish that stand the heat of the day, because she expected his sermon and the singing of psalms to last well into eventide.

Matthew, who did not know this, wrote down the story, alleging that we fed the whole crowd of many hundreds with the seven loaves of bread and the few little fishes we brought for ourselves. Subsequently, all scribes who followed him wrote of this miracle of the fishes, and the size of the multitude fed that night grew with each retelling. These writers were competing with each other to present the good deeds of Yeshua as miraculous events in order to please Peter and Paul, who wanted to convince everyone that Yeshua was none other than the Messiah who will free us from the bondage of all evil.

I tell you this only to make you understand: What is written down by several men of the same bias is hardly truer than what is committed to writing by one who has only one purpose: to reveal the truth. Even the best intentioned fable can in time come to imperil multitudes by setting people against people, again and again.

About My Well-Meaning Intention and Fearful Visions of the Future

I would, therefore, like to shed true light on how Barabbas was liberated from Pilate's prison, why and how he was freed by Yeshua at his own peril. I must tell you the truth, because in my meditations on things to come I have seen disasters born of the story as it had been written down and copied many times over, placing the blame for the crucifixion of our master collectively on us, Jews. I have seen in my haunting visions the many fratricides that the stories conceived to please Rome and the Roman-pagan multitudes that Peter and Paul gathered into their flock will bring.

The stories that now serve to appease many by absolving Pilate from the charge of deicide will lead to fratricides, multiplying and then multiplying again in number as the stories of the true witnesses passed from mouth to mouth fade beyond a whisper and the immutable words of the scrolls become unchallengeable.

But I also see beyond these fearful images to a time when people seeking reconciliation will want to hear the truth, which does not place the blame for the suffering of our Master on the Jews and their high priests, nor on Rome and her Hegemon: This is the true story of the release of Barabbas.

Part II
Events Preceding
Our Arrival in
Jerusalem

Part II
Events Preceding
Our Arrival in
Jerusalem

The Celebration under Roman Occupation of the Escape from Egyptian Captivity

There are those who question whether the sons of Israel ever slaved in Egypt. I do not take sides in this, but understand that the story of their miraculous release by striking fear in the heart of the Pharaoh was used hundreds of years later in Babylon by the high priests and Levites, who feared that the wealthiest Jews, who maintained them by their tithes, would get absorbed into the many peoples of the center of all commerce, arts, and wealth on the shores of the Euphrates and would never return to Jerusalem unless frightened into it by the revenging angel of God who set fear even in the heart of the great Pharaoh.

Not surprisingly, those who returned to the much poorer Judea did not celebrate their escape from Babylon. Instead, they celebrated the miraculous liberation of their ancestors from Egypt, which by then had been shrouded in the mists of miraculous and divine interventions well worth recollection even many centuries later, under Roman occupation. Thousands made their Passover pilgrimage to Jerusalem every year from all parts of Judea – and even from lands much farther away.

The Warring of the Jews among Themselves and against the Romans

Under Roman governance, the Jews of Judea were far from living in bondage, yet they were less free in their divisiveness among themselves than they had been centuries earlier in Babylon. There were those who were content; after all, the Romans built roads where travelers once had had to fear quicksand; they built aqueducts and reservoirs to provide ample water for the city, where before there had barely been enough for ritual washing; and their legions secured peace for the region, allowing commerce to flourish, if perhaps not quite equaling the prosperity of Babylon. And, as you may know if you have a bent for history, opposing these contented men were those who would give their lives to drive out the Romans.

I cannot know how far in the future it will be when you, the finder of these truths, will read my words, nor what will be common knowledge, and what will have been covered by the sands of time. Yet I assume that you know of the bloody war that broke out more than a generation after our Master was last seen in the regions where he once shared the teachings that brought solace to so many. He was not around to preempt the war that brought us defeat at a very high price. You may not know, however, about the uprising that would have broken out thirty some years earlier had our Master not stopped it at the cost of much suffering to himself.

But I must not get ahead of myself. Let me start my account of the honest truth with something you must have heard, since it is mentioned, though not exactly as it happened, in the gospel-histories of our time: The leader of the Zealots, Jeshaua bar Abbas, otherwise known as Barabbas, was arrested just before Passover of the year I am recounting.

Yeshua Finds Out from Judas that Barabbas Is in Prison

After his arrest, Barabbas was not brought before Pilate because his captors believed the man, dressed like a beggar and skulking in the city by night, to be no more than a common thief. Judas Iscariot wanted to bring this news swiftly to our Master, knowing that Barabbas had been his closest friend since childhood in Nazareth. He wanted to assure Yeshua that his friend was safe as long as Pilate did not learn about his role as leader of the Zealots.

Judas also needed to inform Yeshua of another disturbing piece of news that he had learned from connections he maintained with members of the newest and bloodiest of Zealot groups. These several dozen resolute and ferocious Zealots hid sharp daggers, *sicas,* under their cloaks – hence some people began to call them Sicarii, after they had extinguished the lives of many a legionnaire in the dark of the night. Judas's name, Iscariot, came from the long-vanished town of Iscario, where his father's family had come from, but many believed that he was related to the Sicarii. He never contested this misunderstanding. Instead, he managed to make some Sicarii believe that he was one of them. He did this because he was the one among us whom Yeshua counted on to ferret out anything that might endanger the peaceful existence in which love should flourish.

Judas Finds Out that the Uprising Planned by the Sicarii Is Doomed

The Master often referred to this much-loved disciple as his eyes and ears. The Iscariot went in this capacity to mingle with Sicarii in order to find out what they intended to do in the absence of Barabbas, their leader. His suspicion that trouble was brewing proved true: the Sicarii were readying to lead the Zealots against their occupiers, mingling into the large crowds of pilgrims entering the city for the high holy day of Passover. They aimed to kill all the legionaries guarding the Tower of Antonia, free Barabbas, capture Pilate, and then negotiate the withdrawal of the Romans from the Holy City.

Judas knew at once that this plan would lead to disaster, as organizing so many men to act secretly and in concert was beyond the competence of Sicarii, who until then had always acted alone against lonely guards.

Filled with apprehension, Judas also went to the inn that was frequented by legionaries, some of whom he often treated to good ales, as he did then, and to good ends, as he had discovered that Pilate was aware of the planned uprising and was secretly reinforcing his guards. Furthermore, Pilate had ordered several hundred well-selected men to dress as pilgrims, mingle with the crowds, and pull their swords out from under their traveling robes when the Zealots revealed themselves. They had been instructed to kill all the rebels and all the pilgrims they suspected to be Zealots or sympathizers.

Judas hurried back to us to tell all he had learned, because he knew that only Yeshua could free his friend, Barabbas, and only Barabbas could stop the doomed uprising.

Yeshua and Judas Lead Us to Jerusalem and Make Plans to Free Barabbas

Knowing how much the Master valued life and loved his friend Barabbas, we weren't surprised at all when he instructed us to pack only the bare essentials so we could travel light and fast to Jerusalem. We two dozen of his closest disciples (including three women: Maria of Magdala and Lazar's sisters, Maria and Marta) started out before Judas could tell the Master all he had learned and they could figure out how to stop the bloodshed.

Peter always believed himself to be the first among us, but to his chagrin, Yeshua signaled Judas to step beside him as we lined up in pairs to travel the narrow paths winding among the rocks of the desert. Yeshua and Judas talked continuously, sometimes in a whisper, but eventually one of them always spoke up so that those behind them could hear and pass what they had said along to the rest of us.

This is how we learned what Yeshua and Judas had agreed on: Barabbas must be freed at any cost. Unlike the rash and fatally impulsive Sicarii, he was a patient man, capable of assessing the odds and waiting until the moment to act arrived. As their leader of many years, he was the only one the Zealots would listen to, even those who had come under the influence of the Sicarii. They also agreed that only Yeshua, his closest friend, could convince Barabbas to call off the bloodshed. To our great anguish, they also agreed that Yeshua could talk to him only if Judas concocted a scheme to get him arrested and thrown into the dungeons of the tower.

Yeshua Recounts His Teachings about the Truest Love as We Anguish over His Fate

As we all cried out in torment, hearing this and imagining the fate that might await our Master, Judas called for a short rest in the shadow of a rock wall to try to calm us down. Judas's efforts were to no avail. The short-tempered Peter (who was always envious when Judas got closer to Yeshua than he) attacked Judas with a ferocity unheard of among us brothers, who had devoted ourselves to perfecting our love for one another. Working up his gall, he called Judas a traitor, spewing profanity, words I could not commit to writing. Finally, Yeshua calmed him down by embracing him, until between sobs Peter turned

away from Judas and addressed his worries –
which we all shared – directly to the Master:

"Judas could surely arrange for you, my
Lord, to be taken into that fearful fortress," he
said, throwing one more dirty look at Judas.
He then continued, "He could even bribe the
guards to put you into your friend's cell, but did
he tell you, as he was whispering into your ear
throughout most of our journey, how he would
get your friend out of the dungeon and save you
as well?"

"He could hardly do that, Peter, but if I stayed
there – " Yeshua couldn't finish his words, for in
our fear for our Master's life we all cried out in
anguish. Yeshua silenced us by raising his hand
and spoke to us thusly: "Have you all forgotten
what I taught you on the Mount of Olives? Have
you forgotten what I taught you about the truest
love?"

John, the youngest, fell to his knees and
clung to the Master's legs, as if longing to hold
him back. As a good disciple, he had to recite
exactly what Yeshua had told us and others,
more than once: "You said, my Lord, you said
that greater love hath no man than this, that a
man lay down his life for his friends."

John was a good disciple; he knew how much
it meant to our Master if we not only quoted one
of his famous sayings, but also cited at least one
of the expositions that usually followed, like the

one he then recounted: "Even if we exemplify perfect love toward everyone throughout our lives, we can lose all if we turn with envy and hate toward those whose time has not yet arrived; if we force the angel of death to pull us out of life by the hair. You also told us that we can experience the most perfect joy as we step out of life if we leave our greatest treasure – our place on earth – lovingly to the generations that follow us under the sun."

Peter Argues against
Yeshua's Plan

"We asked you then when we should do so,"
interjected Peter, "and you answered: when its time
has come. But you still have much to do, Master,
to ensure that the words of the prophets foretelling
the deeds of the Messiah are fulfilled."

"My time has come, Peter!" answered Yeshua,
impatiently, as he had snapped ever more often
as Peter and his supporters tried to convince
him that he was the anointed one who will save
us from the four horsemen and the beasts of the
apocalypse.

In vain had the Master reminded them
that the Torah does not make any mention of
a Messiah, and even according to the better
prophecies, we can only expect the coming of
an Anointed One when people everywhere have
learned to love one another.

Yeshua Explains Why He Is Ready to Die for His Friends, and Reminds Us of the Sufferings of His Childhood

In spite of my sorrow, I was not surprised when I heard the Master address us thusly. "If I must give my life to free Barabbas, I shall die happily, Peter. He has stood by my side, when everyone else turned away from me, the *mamzer* – worse, one hundred times worse than a bastard born before wedlock. A *mamzer,* who, according to the Torah and our customs, everyone had to shun. My friend Barabbas never scorned me, even when everyone else had turned away from me, the rotten fruit of an assumed adultery."

It was not the first time that Yeshua had talked to us with such bitterness of the sufferings of his childhood. When it became known that he had not been begotten by Joseph, and his mother never uttered the name of the man who sired him, the people of Nazareth could only assume that the young virgin of great beauty had charmed a married man who had grown tired of his wife of too many years. Mary, the mother of Yeshua, should have been stoned to death as an adulteress for her resolute silence.

However, the people of Nazareth forwent this punishment, given that by the time it came to light that Joseph was not the father of Yeshua Mary had born him several children who did not deserve the punishment of seeing their mother's body corrupted. But they considered Yeshua a *mamzer* who, according to traditions and the words of the Torah, must be shunned by all.

I recount this because Yeshua told us many times that he was an outcast in search of his father, longing for his love and wanting to love him; and this deep love accumulated in him, and it is of this love we have all partaken.

We Receive Consolation and Guidance while Discussing Other Ways to Free Barabbas

"We understand, Lord, and we know your great love for Barabbas. Still, couldn't Judas contrive something to spare you the sorrow of giving your life in order to save your friend?" Simon, the former Zealot, asked bitterly. "We also need you."

"My words will remain with you, Simon. Let us think now on how we can get Barabbas out of Pilate's dungeon. We don't know what's happened there since Judas brought us news of this futile and dangerous plot. In order to prevent the outbreak of such an uprising, which would lead to the certain death of hundreds of Zealots and legionaries who are also good people, Barabbas needs to hear all of what Judas learned of Pilate's plans. But he must hear this from someone in whose every word he believes. Who else could that be but I? Although I know that our friend from Iscariot would love to go in my stead. Is that not right, Judas?"

Judas, struggling with tears, could only nod.

"And what if you don't manage to rescue Barabbas? What if you sacrifice yourself in vain, Master?" Peter besieged Yeshua with his questions. But then, he believed that he had found a way out: "Perhaps Judas could get Barabbas to write a message to his men ..."

"We can sew gold into your cloak to pay off the guards and a stylus for Barabbas to write a command to stop his Zealots." Judas sounded as though he was thinking aloud. "And then, if you can convince Pilate that you don't want to be king of anyone, you can smuggle it out, he will let you free after a mandatory flogging. And getting you in is assured" – Judas's voice broke – "if we can convince the Prefect that you want to be the king of the Jews. His people, who are most certainly watching us from afar even now, won't let you out of their sight for a moment once we enter the city."

Yeshua Entrusts Us to the Wisdom of Judas

"What shall we do, Master?" asked John – the youngest one among us – "How will we, who have always followed you, know what to do when you are no longer among us? Tell us what to do and we shall do as you say." Kneeling and raising Yeshua's right hand to his forehead, John made this pledge in all our names, and Yeshua raised His voice to speak to us:

"Always do as Judas advises. Follow his example in everything. He has his sources and will always know what is happening in the fortress. Do not reach for weapons to rise like heroes beside me. My mission ends here. Yours is only beginning."

Peter always assumed the place of leader if the Master was not with us for more than a few hours. Yeshua did not seem to mind, nor did we. On those occasions we had nothing to fear, no decisions had to be made, and we did not need anyone to look out for us. John asked his questions because he knew full well – as did we all – that in the precarious situation in which we found ourselves, we needed more than someone who likes to play leader. We needed someone who would always know or could find out what was happening and how we could avoid impending peril. Judas Iscariot was the only such man among us, even if he had never shown any inclination to be anything other than one of us. If he had distinguished himself in something, it was his humbleness and his readiness to serve without expectation of reward. I am ashamed to say that the rest of us were fulfilled by being close to Yeshua, and as I seek to be honest, I must admit that we accepted all he did for us, but it never so much as occurred to us that we might need to do something for him.

Peter Is Angered by the Elevation of Judas

We assured Yeshua that we would do as he instructed us – all of us, that is, except Peter and a few of those whom he had recruited not long before. They pulled away from us and put their heads together, obviously planning to protest, but seeing this, Yeshua said to them: "You can turn away from me, Peter, you can deny me from before the cock crow until the sun sets, but I will never deny my love for you. I know your big heart, which you believe capable of greater love than the others, and if you feel it so, it may be so, but now you will all need someone with a sharp and cunning mind to outwit those we are up against."

Yeshua said a few more words to ease the pang of Peter's disappointment, but he was undeniably still sulking, as he returned to us only after Judas had told us that he must arrive in Jerusalem before us to arrange our welcoming, and hurried away.

Soon thereafter, we lined up to get going again. Yeshua asked Peter to walk beside him, and He talked with him most of the way to Jerusalem. As the city appeared on the horizon, we started to sing psalms as pilgrims always do. We hoped that this would calm the quick-tempered Peter, but as we later learned, he never overcame the animosity he harbored for Judas.

Part III
The Loyalty of Judas and the Untrue Story of His Demise

Part III
The Loyalty of Judas and the Untrue Story of His Demise

Remembering how we sang to ease our sorrow and anxiety while making our way toward Jerusalem, my mind keeps echoing a line of one of our favored psalms: "My mouth shall speak of wisdom; and the meditation of my heart shall be of understanding." I pray another psalm for humbleness in my task: "Lead me in thy truth, and teach me: for thou art the God of my salvation; on thee do I wait all the day." That reminds me of yet another verse: "O spare me, that I may recover strength, before I go hence, and be no more." And as I see us making our way toward the gates of Jerusalem, I realize that in some far-away future days you will know us no better than we know the past that gave birth to those psalms, which some of our rabbis spend their lives interpreting.

Much as I dislike interrupting the flow of the story that I have to tell you, I must make clear that in spite of whatever odium you in your time have learned about Judas, he was faithful to the Master and his teachings until his very last breath, when he was martyred for the cause he had served. Before you can accept the truths about Yeshua's self-sacrifice, I must reveal to you the true self of Judas, freeing him from the false image I assume you have inherited from those Gospels that were written to please Paul and were allowed to survive into posterity.

It is not easy for me to share with you all that I must to make credible what has been hidden from you. These truths were also successfully hidden from most of us who lived in the time it happened or immediately after. So let me get over the worst of what I must say; let me take you *in medias res,* as our Roman friends would say, right into the heart of the matter: I must tell you that the rumors that Judas betrayed Yeshua to Caiaphas – as I assume you learned to be a fact – were started by something Peter had said. When, to our greatest sorrow, we received word of Judas's death, Peter remarked that surely the Iscariot's bad conscience had driven him to kill himself. Nothing could be further from the truth: His body was found hanged from a tree for all to see, but with a Sicarus dagger in his heart and a tablet hanging from it with one single word written on it in blood: TRAITOR. There can be no doubt that the Sicarri learned that Judas had conferred with Pilate and arranged to free Barabbas, who had stopped their plot. By the time we buried Judas, word of his suicide had spread so far and wide that we, his true friends, could not convince anyone of what really had happened.

Peter Denies
Knowing Yeshua

Why did Peter's friends spread falsehoods about Judas? Not out of sheer animosity, that I can assure you. Yet I cannot imagine why anyone would have wanted to present Judas as the betrayer of Yeshua other than those who wanted to draw attention away from the sad fact that Peter not once, but three times, betrayed the Master. Since it happened in front of many people in the Sanhedrin, it could not be denied. It is mentioned in most of the Gospels, but not in the weighty manner in which it actually happened. According to the version of the story that, gaining Paul's approval, was preserved, a damsel and two other people of no consequence asked Peter if he knew the Nazarene, and it was only to them that he denied his Master.

This is how it happened. When the high priest Caiaphas called on Peter to testify on behalf of the Nazarene against his accusers, Peter was so scared that he denied even knowing him. Peter was asked thrice, once by each member of the tribunal, as custom had it, and Peter denied him thrice. Everyone in Jerusalem heard of Peter's denial, but everybody who was not there when it happened heard it differently. Soon most people started to believe what Peter's friends — the handful of younger men he brought into the fold of disciples — wanted them to believe, and this is the version of the story that went into the Gospel of Matthew about that curious damsel. But Peter's friends were afraid that in spite of this not very well crafted but generally accepted false version of Peter's denial, the truth might come to light. This is why they needed to find someone whom they could build up as a villain of such treachery that he would fulfill the people's need for someone to scorn.

One Mendacity
Leads to Another

This fabricated account of Judas's deceit was the poisonous seed that grew into that false account of Yeshua's mortification, which has already set the younger brother against the older brother and will undoubtedly lead to even more heinous discord in the future. I had to tell you all this because, whether or not the false stories about Judas stemmed from Peter's animosity toward him, I must assume that they reached you through the Gospels, which gave them credence. As we know, murky gloom is seen darker and darker as night falls, just as even the faintest rays of glory shine brighter and brighter as the light of day returns. I dread to think that Judas will become, with the passage of time, the embodiment of evil so that you may find it hard to give credence to what I have already told you about him and what I must still tell you.

You may think it is some personal animosity on my part that leads me to assume that vicious rumors were started by Peter's people. I can assure you that this is not the case. I would not even mind if Peter and Paul had established their own teachings, not mentioning Yeshua, but, as it is, they found it more expedient to base their church of heavenly glory on our humble Master, who is no longer with us, and can thus be made larger than life: The Messiah.

Actually, because Peter and Paul are so different, it is hard for me to mention them in the same breath. Peter is the simple-minded fisherman, still casting his net and not minding who he catches in it, Jews or Gentiles, devout Mithras followers or pagans, Romans or barbarians. In contrast, Paul was by far the best-educated of us disciples in Rome, and the strongest willed. He always had the last word in any debate, managing to convince everyone on both sides of the Tiberis that he knew more about Yeshua than anyone else, even though he had never met him except in that apparition I mentioned to you. It was then that an image of the Master sprang out of his head as, according to the faith of the Greeks, Athena sprang from the head of Zeus, fully clad in armor with her shield and spear ready in hand.

Paul was not a follower of Yeshua as we, his true disciples, were. He created for himself a Jesus whose human greatness was recognized by the Roman governor of Judea more readily than it was by us faithful Jews. Paul liked the story of John, according to which Pontius Pilate pointed to Yeshua when they were standing in front of a jeering crowd and said, *"Ecce Homo, behold the man."* In fact, Pilate never said that. John put those words into the Hegemon's mouth, knowing full well they were the ones the Lord had said in ancient times, introducing to Samuel that Saul who was to free Israel from Philistine subjugation. John put these words into his Gospel, as he put in everything he could to shore up his contention that Yeshua is the Messiah who will deliver his people from Roman occupation and all other evil. To the contrary, however, the essence of Yeshua's teaching was that we, each one of us, must redeem *ourselves,* through love, understanding, and compassion. He lived according to what he preached, as you will see for yourself as I return to the story of our arrival in Jerusalem.

Part IV
The Freeing of
Barabbas and
Yeshua's Last Days
in Jerusalem

Our Arrival and
Welcome into the City

Judas arranged for Yeshua to be greeted by crowds as we entered Jerusalem. He even borrowed a donkey from someone, because Peter insisted that Yeshua must fulfill a prophecy about the Messiah riding into the Holy City on some beast of burden, and he wanted to see all such prophecies fulfilled. Judas was eager to please Peter. Indeed, he pleased all of us.

We were welcomed into the city with a shower of Hosannas, loud enough to raise Pilate from his afternoon slumber. This achieved its intended purpose of capturing everyone's attention: Judas saw one or two spies leave the crowd from time to time to make their way to the Tower of Antonia. As we neared it, the crowd recruited by Judas, hailed Yeshua as the King of the Jews.

The next day we were busy making arrangements for Passover dinner. Yeshua and Judas managed to get a room in the overcrowded city on the second level of a large house belonging to a man who had listened to the Master's sermons many times.

Arrangements Are Made
for the Passover Meal

Disguised as a man for precaution, Mary Magdalene went with Simon and John to get provisions. Judas was worried that Pilate's agents might abduct her, assuming that they could extract more easily from a woman the reasons for our noisy reception into the city, or, if they recognized her, might even capture her to use her as bait to catch Yeshua.

The Master wanted to be caught, but not yet – and not on Pilate's terms, but on Judas's, who felt it important to convince Pilate's men that Yeshua was on a mission of importance. He even arranged to get a mysterious man carrying a large jug of water to lead us to the house where we planned to have the supper. The sight of a man doing a woman's job would be conspicuous enough to ensure that we would be followed and watched.

The Supper and the Taunting of Pilate's Spies

To Peter's chagrin, Yeshua seated Mary Magdalene to his right at the supper. I sat next to Mary, but it would have been rude to have eavesdropped on their conversation. Most of the time they whispered to each other so Pilate's men would not hear them in the noise of the merriment. Judas, on the other hand, spoke loudly, saying incriminating things about prophecies of the return of David's descendent to the throne of Judea, knowing full well that Pilate's spies were within earshot.

Yeshua, unable to resist taunting them, rose toward the end of the supper to silence us, and, giving us all a sly look, said: "There is a traitor among you!"

Restraining our laughter, we asked, "Which of us is it, Master?"

And he said even louder: "The one to whom I offer bread." And with that, he gave Judas a piece of bread dipped in wine. We all knew, of course, that he did that to aggravate those who could only hear, but not see us. We knew that Yeshua was not serious, since among his faithful disciples, Judas was the one who, as Yeshua's eyes and ears, had had innumerable occasions to prove his unwavering dedication to the Master.

Although the truth about Barabbas's liberation has been forgotten by most, this should not be attributed to the imperfection of human memory. You would be right to conclude from what you've learned so far that certain accounts have been deliberately distorted, in no small measure by Paul's Rome-loving followers, who sought to deflect the blame of deicide from Pilate and place it on the Jews. As a first-hand witness to these events, I can tell you exactly how the story was rewritten to this end. So let me set the record straight.

What Actually Befell Us as Opposed to What Came to Be Written

It's true that Yeshua was soon taken captive and that a great crowd gathered when his case was heard. It is true that many shouted loudly, "Crucify the Nazarene," but each and every one of them was Pilate's hired man.

It's true that there were many who roared at the appropriate time, "Let Barabbas free!" But this had been organized by Judas.

Not a soul there spoke his own mind.

It's true that some of our high priests were present at the hearing, because Pilate charged Yeshua with blasphemy rather than treason, which would have required him to try and put to death all of his companions as well. In blasphemy cases, Pilate let the chief rabbis pass judgment and washed his hands of all blame even if he told them what verdict to reach. If I may say, the idea is laughable that Pilate, the all powerful procurator of Rome, was afraid of a few dozen unarmed Jews who were shouting, "Crucify him, crucify the Nazarene," as John would have us believe.

In short: It's untrue — and is simply unbelievable — that the crowd forced the all-powerful governor to crucify Yeshua, who had so enriched their lives and whom they had come to love. The truth is quite different.

Judas Has to Change His Plans to Forestall the Bloodshed

Let me backtrack a bit. Soon after the Master's capture, Judas learned that he had not been taken to Fort Antonia. The Jewish high priests, whom Pilate needed to pass the judgment he had ordered, would never have set foot in a place laden with statues of pagan gods and certainly not the day before the high holy day of Passover. Thus, Yeshua could not have met Barabbas.

Judas had to devise a new plan:

He let slip to a Roman mercenary friend of his that it was he to whom the Nazarene had handed the bread at the Passover supper. Pilate immediately summoned Judas, who disclosed to the Prefect the true reason for all their doings, as he saw no other way at that point to save both Yeshua and Barabbas and stop the revolt. And he judged the matter even more urgent than he had the day before, because he had learned that the legionaries had received orders to spare neither the innocent pilgrims nor the inhabitants of Jerusalem with whom the Zealots planned to mingle.

He therefore disclosed to Pilate that the imprisoned Barabbas was a childhood friend of Yeshua, and Yeshua sought to free him, even at the cost of his own life, to prevent the uprising.

Pilate Convinces Himself that Judas's Words Are True

Pilate was a battle-hardened man, but he knew that Rome had not sent him to Judea to suppress rebellions, but rather to preempt them. He believed what Judas Iscariot had told him, because he had had him followed on many occasions and knew that he was working for Yeshua, the wayfarer rabbi from Nazareth who was also known as the prophet of love and peace and as an orator capable of attracting great throngs of people.

So it came to pass that the Prefect placed the two friends in the same hold in the dungeon and had someone stand in secret by its door to overhear their every word. Some even claimed that Pilate himself put his noble ear to that door. When he was convinced that Barabbas would listen to his friend and would prevent the hopeless rebellion, Pilate decided to have him released. However, he had to make it appear that this was on account of the Passover tradition of releasing a prisoner chosen by the crowd each year.

Pilate did not meet Barabbas, nor did he send to him an emissary. He let him and everyone else believe that he was being released to comply with the tradition of yielding to the wishes of the people. He made sure that nothing would jeopardize Barabbas's credibility before the Zealots. The Procurator – the survivor of many intrigues in Rome and the instigator of others – must have known full well that it would be the end of Barabbas and of any hope to preempt the revolt if the Zealots were to suspect that he had made a deal to get out.

Yeshua and Judas Arrange with Pilate the Terms of Barabbas's Release

On the other hand, the Hegemon not only entered into hard bargaining with Yeshua, but as we later learned, he had already worked out the framework of a deal with Judas even before he met the Master and had convinced himself that through his friend, Barabbas, he might be able to prevent the revolt. The core of the agreement achieved by Judas was that Pilate would spare Yeshua's life if on the first three days after Passover there was no attack against his men. But to keep up appearances until then, Yeshua would have to subjugate himself to all the punishments to which his friend would have been sentenced, including the agonies and humiliation of the flogging and crucifixion.

Yeshua accepted these terms, without a word of complaint – and not just to assure that no one would question the reason for his friend's release.

Yeshua's Reasons for Not Trying to Escape Crucifixion

Yeshua had mentioned several times to those of us who did not want to make him into the Messiah that he wanted to be reborn to what he was when we first met. Before Peter took upon himself to gather every word that was ever written about the Messiah and tried to get Yeshua to fulfill every one of those prophecies. What distressed the Master the most about such badgering was that he himself had almost come to believe that he was the Anointed One. To free himself of this delusion, he wanted to be reborn through the rite of death and resurrection that had allowed Lazarus to start a new life.

He wanted to return not as the celebrated orator known for his often over-interpreted parables and allegedly miraculous healings, which bred increasingly high expectations that were increasingly difficult to satisfy. And – as he confessed to some of us who understood his predicament – he was also afraid of falling prey to the temptations of vanity, for as the talk of the coming of the Messiah had begun getting out of hand, he himself had begun to feel conceited vainglory creeping up on him.

It was through the humiliating experience of the flogging and crucifixion that Yeshua hoped to be reborn as the humble person he had used to be, whom we all had loved.

In addition, Yeshua also wanted to be reborn so that he would finally be released from the humiliation of being a *mamzer*. Because of this stigma, he had been unable to marry Mary Magdalene, who herself did not have an unblemished past, but was at least not a *mamzer*.

Yeshua could have married a woman in Samaria, and indeed he almost did before he met Mary, but in Judea, which adhered more strictly to the Torah, a *mamzer* could only marry another *mamzer*, one born of adultery or begotten of a father unnamed and as such, supposedly as a result of adultery. Thus he, the embodiment of love, was not able to experience the blessings of the love that only marriage can offer.

Pilate Fulfills His Terms

Judas relayed to us Pilate's pledge to spare
Yeshua's life and the Master's acceptance of
what might befall him, even crucifixion. I do
not have to tell you that we spent the following
three days praying that Barabbas would succeed
in restraining his men. Judas did more: He met
with several Zealots to spread rumors that would
underscore the hopelessness of their cause. He
contrived details, such as his contention that
in addition to the several hundred selected
legionaries already smuggled into Jerusalem to
slaughter the rebels, a whole legion was under
way to recapture the city in the unlikely case
that it fall to the Zealots and Sicarii and make
the rebels pay for their insurrection.

I have described to the best of my knowledge
the framework of the agreement between Judas
and Pilate. But let me restate it here point by

point so you can compare it with what was bequeathed to posterity by Paul's scribes:

Yeshua would be flogged until blood was shed for all to see. He would carry the *pantibulum* of the cross amidst jeering men and women (Pilate always had crowds of people ready either to cheer or jeer at his beckoning). His shinbones would not be broken so as not to cause his death. The lancer would draw blood, but would not endanger his life.

According to custom and the laws of the Sabbath, the body would be taken down before sunset and entombed.

The most trustworthy centurion of the Hegemon would oversee the safe execution of these terms.

This centurion would also post trustworthy men to guard the tomb.

If, during the first three days of Passover, no uprising broke out, the soldiers would remove the Procurator's seal and roll away the boulder that closed off the mouth of the tomb. Yeshua would be left to his fate.

And this is how it happened: There was no rebellion, and the Prefect kept his word. Yeshua was nursed back to health by Mary Magdalene, who had hurried to the tomb on the third day.

The Rebirth of the Yeshua
We Met at Lake Galilee

After three days in the solitude of the tomb, Yeshua was truly reborn to become what he wanted to be: the one I had met not much more than two years earlier standing on the shores of the Sea of Galilee. He stood there, silently radiating so much love that all three of us in the boat had been drawn to him irresistibly. (I must clarify that neither Simon – the Peter that I have been mentioning – nor his brother, Andrew, had been there. They met Yeshua more than a year later, despite Peter's fervently spread claim that he was the Master's first disciple – or Apostle, as he began to say after he learned this word from Luke the Greek).

After his rebirth, Yeshua even looked different, much more as I remembered him from the time we first met. Though his face looked gaunt after his ordeal, the same love radiated from his eyes that had burned his visage into my heart. He looked so much like the humble, loving Yeshua of days long past that those who had prophesied his coming as the Messiah failed to recognize him on the road to Emmaus. In Emmaus, they thought I was crazed when I pointed to his still unhealed wounds and assured those crowded into the house – trembling with fear like sheep that have lost their shepherd – that a real flesh and blood man stood before us, and he was none other than our beloved Master.

The Testament of
the Witness

I have written this testament in good faith, hoping that whoever should someday find this honest account of the Master's last days among us will have the courage to read it and share it with others. But if I can beg your indulgence a little longer, let me say the following, so as to not leave any loose ends:

Pressured by Paul's "disciples," Peter and his followers did all they could to have me silenced in Rome. I could not address the multitudes they drew to hear of the teachings and deeds of the Master, whom they started to call Our Lord, an epithet that would have been most abhorrent to him, for he had always said that no one should be raised above any other man or woman, or even child, as we were all created in the image of the same God. He never let us call him "Rabbi" as he knew himself to be a *mamzer* and did not want to offend the rabbis who came from impeccable families. In his humility he referred to himself often as "son of man," so as not to elevate himself above any of us.

My Futile Objections to Calling Yeshua the Christ

Yeshua had allowed us to call him Master when we sought his attention, not just for friendly banter but for guidance on the many possible interpretations of some of his parables. Later, he got used to us calling him Master all the time. But he never let us call him Messiah, and some of us later objected to him being thusly named in the scriptures. Peter understood our reasons and Paul – who also knew that in the Torah not even the anointed ones are called by this name – made the scribes rewrite the word Messiah to read Christ. This is the Latin way of writing the Greek word *Khristos,* which also means something like anointed, but at least Yeshua would have understood it, since he spoke a little Greek, like most of us who occasionally had to deal with legionaries.

My objections to the use of the word Christ
fell on deaf ears. In fact, soon most of the new
disciples said Jesus Christ, as though it were
a name. And I was silenced, so without me to
contradict them, they could lead their fold in
Rome to believe that the Messiah had come in
the person of Yeshua, though there was not so
much as a single sign of this, as was clearly
demonstrated in the days of Emperor Nero, when
many people became more evil than ever before.
And there was no Messiah to come to our aid
when we lined up around the Temple to prevent
its desecration with the statue of Caligula.

My Expression of Good Wishes for Well-Deserved Bliss and Much Happiness to Yeshua of Nazareth and Mary of Magdala

As you perhaps know, soon after all this came to pass, Yeshua disappeared. According to Peter and the other believers in the arrival of the Messiah in the person of Yeshua, he ascended to heaven. How, they didn't know. No one saw him soaring into the blue yonder on Elijah's chariot of fire.

Yeshua had seen, however, how disappointed most of his disciples had been when he had not returned as the Savior to liberate them from Roman domination, and he had never liked to disappoint anyone. This might have been one reason for his disappearance.

There is no trace of Mary Magdalene either. I hope there is some truth to the story according to which she and Yeshua were accompanied to a faraway place somewhere in Gallia by the same centurion who watched over Yeshua's life in Calvary and had his tomb guarded for three days. I hope and pray that they found there the happiness and most perfect love that they so richly deserve.

Part V
My Parting Words
to the Reader

I hope and believe that this account, written anonymously and in hiding, will someday reach the hands and hearts of people who dare to accept the truths encrusted in these words, even if it is against the established teachings.

In old age, having finally won my peace, I remain lovingly yours,

– Anonymous

Contents

CPSIA information can be obtained
at www.ICGtesting.com
Printed in the USA
LVHW101644301121
704862LV00014B/358/J